Turning

poems by

Diane Henningfeld

Finishing Line Press
Georgetown, Kentucky

Turning

Copyright © 2016 by Diane Henningfeld
ISBN 978-1-944251-81-9 First Edition
All rights reserved under International and Pan-American Copyright Conventions. No part of this book may be reproduced in any manner whatsoever without written permission from the publisher, except in the case of brief quotations embodied in critical articles and reviews.

ACKNOWLEDGMENTS

"Snatches" first appeared in *Storm Cellar*.
"October" was published by *The Michigan Poet* as a broadsheet and online.
"December" first appeared in *The Penwood Review*.
"Turning" and "Wisconsin Triolet" were published in *Dunes Review*.

The line "Do not forsake me, oh my darling" used in my poem "Andrews Shopping Center: 1968" is from "The Ballad of High Noon," the theme song of the movie High Noon, dating from 1952, with words by Ned Washington, and music by Dmitri Tiomkin. It was sung by Tex Ritter over the opening credits of the movie.

Editor: Christen Kincaid

Cover Art: Don Cellini, www.doncellini.com

Author Photo: Char-Lene Wilkins

Cover Design: Elizabeth Maines

Printed in the USA on acid-free paper.
Order online: www.finishinglinepress.com
also available on amazon.com

Author inquiries and mail orders:
Finishing Line Press
P. O. Box 1626
Georgetown, Kentucky 40324

Table of Contents

1	Michigan Left
2	Turning
3	October
4	Visitation
7	December
8	Saint Machar's in the Rain
9	New Year's Eve 1999: Grand Marais
10	Easter Wings
11	On Sundays
12	Andrews Shopping Center: 1968
13	Wisconsin Triolet: My Future Mother-in-Law Teaches Me to Play Sheepshead
14	Live Trap
15	True Confessions
16	Sault Ste. Marie
17	Aberdeen, Midwinter
18	Haar on Don Street
19	The Mathematics of Seeing You Again
21	"Shall I Compare Thee to a Summer's Day?" You Ask
22	February
23	Snatches
25	It's Not Over

To Ken, Kate, and Anne

Michigan Left

Sometimes in Michigan,
you have to turn right
to go left, turn north to go south,
and then you make a U-turn
to get to where you want to go.

And all the time I thought
we were traveling
in the same direction.

Turning

In March, we drag the stoneboat
through the fields and gather rocks
turned up by frost. Dad's gone.
Rabecki rents the eighty acres

for his oats and beans.
Mother lives alone. She says
she'll never leave the farm.
We turn our eyes away, and keep

the farmyard neat: no broken
plows, or rusty cars, or tools.
The stones we pile behind
the shed, like promises to Dad

we meant to keep. Now,
there's nothing we can keep for long,
not barn, not house, not stones.
We gather at the farm in late

November, raking leaves
wept down by aching oaks. Our bundled
kids run wild across
the lawn and burrow in the leaves

like woodchucks seeking shelter
for their winter sleep. At dusk
we light the bonfire, warm
our hands, talk about the price

of wheat, and drink our bitter
German beer. The sparks fly upward.
High above, migrant
geese form cryptic hieroglyphs.

Mother says she talks to ghosts.
The stones are silent, still.

October

We never used the front door at our house,
always preferring to slip in through the side door,
an indirect route through the kitchen

to the living room, the living room where
my father slipped into death, as I held his hand and said,
Don't worry, Daddy, don't worry. We'll be all right.

And though we were not all right, not at all,
my father used my assurance
to slip out of the living room,

his last exhalation dispersing
into the air of the house,
as we inhaled and impossibly continued

living. Later, they took him out the front door,
the most direct route to the hearse waiting in the drive.
And my mother moved the furniture

and vacuumed the floor, so that when I slipped in
from the kitchen, my wild grief silently contained,
it was as if my father had never been

in the living room at all, except for the front door,
standing open to an October breeze,
passing softly through the house.

Visitation

1. *The Deer*

I did not see the deer
until I nearly stumbled
across her head.
Although the flies
had not yet started their communion,
I could not meet her eye.

2. *Disposal of the Dead*

Burial:
with or without embalming;
in a compostable cardboard box;
in gold-plated, velvet-lined coffin;
deep or shallow grave, marked or unmarked.

Cremation:
direct, no embalming;
post-funeral, with embalming;
eco-cremation, with dental fillings removed;
on a pyre; in an oven;
on a boat laden with gold and silver.

Placement of the Ashes:
tossed from an airplane;
skyrocketed in fireworks;
encapsulated in memorial jewelry;
settled in an urn in front of the fireplace;
stashed in a box at the back of a closet.

Excarnation:
Comanche burial platforms;
Tibetan sky burial, with axes and vultures;
Zoarastrian Towers of Silence.

3. *Something About the Dead*

There is something about the dead
that does not want to be deposed.

We smell their cologne in crowded rooms,
see them pinching the fruit in grocery stores.
When we pick up the phone,
we hear their voices in the dial tone.

The dead want to hang around the house,
go with us to the movies.
They want us to dust their knick-knacks,
keep their pictures on the mantle,
cook their favorite meals,
invite them to birthday parties and weddings,
balance their checkbooks,
account for their sins.

The dead demand our full attention.

4. *Dia de los Muerto*s

The dead move around the house
like the lost wind, whispering names
left behind. The house quakes, trembles.

We throw open doors and windows,
we welcome the dead, bake
cakes and cookies, make coffee.

Our *ofrendas* hold sugar skulls and candles.
We offer libations to the dead who arrive
sounding like butterfly wings

and dry leaves on the wind.
The dead fill the house with visions
that trouble our dreams.

We ask them for stories of where
they've been, but the dead
are not disposed to answer.

5. *The Eyes of the Dead*

Closed with silver coins
to pay the ferryman's toll,
or to shield the living
from what they might see
mirrored there.

A deer. Her eye.
A silver coin.

December

After the Christmas lamb has been
resurrected as St. Stephen's stew
after the bags are packed and loaded,
the silver van backs out
of the drive in a flurry
of waving hands and airy kisses
the house, so briefly transfigured
by these days of grace, grows quiet

as death. We perform our lonely offices:
I struggle with the bed linens,
he vacuums the floor.
We collect sacred offerings
left behind: a toy truck
under the television,
a blankie behind a pillow. And I think,
soon we will become extraneous.

We are fading. Soon, we will drowse
on someone else's sofa as other hands
prepare the Christmas roast,
the New Year's shrimp, the Easter ham.
We will nod and watch
other people's children open gifts.
We soon will be impossible
to buy presents for, so they will wrap body

lotion, stamps, and chocolates.
They will need us less at family
rituals and though we will be
the honored guests at the final,
inevitable sacrament,
we will not attend. I turn
my hospital corner, tight as a shroud.
I turn my hope toward Easter.

Saint Machar's in the Rain

Saint Machar's stately spires tower high
and dark above the poets and the priests,
the Calvinists and Catholics alike deceased,
the sleeping dead of Aberdeen who lie
beneath this ancient churchyard. What remains
of all their passions and their grief? Dunbar
sore lamented for the passing of the makars,
those scribes who thought their words and names
would stand as sturdy monuments. Few
have been remembered. Words unread now line
their crumbling tombs, obscured by rain and time,
while Dunbar's orison floats ghostly through
the mist: *Timor mortis conturbat me.*
My footprints melt, like words I meant to say.

New Year's Eve 1999
Grand Marais

Snow falls lightly on Superior,
and thin white clouds
scud in front of the moon.
The big lake moves to
its own dark and inscrutable rhythms.

You hold champagne in one hand,
the coming year in the other.
You know it takes resolution
to dress in the morning,
put on makeup, a fresh smile,
and you know there are more
New Year's Eves behind you now
than are to come.

Someone sings "Auld Lang Syne."
You raise your glass to the waves,
and think about a boy
you used to know. Tomorrow
is soon enough for resolution.

Far out on Superior,
a freighter's single light,
moving slowly west.

Easter Wings

Overnight the landscape
changes from budding spring
to grey and white,
trees and houses blurred
with fog and muffled silence.
The river, invisible below,
flows with preternatural quiet.

Then overhead, a rush of air
like angels passing,
white forms in white fog,
wild swans, so close
the wind from their wings
graces my upturned face.

On Sundays

we went to my Grandfather Andrews'
big white house on Washington Avenue
in downtown Warren, Ohio,
to watch *Bonanza* on his color TV.
Pa and the Cartwright boys had skin
the color of lizards, but even so, I thought Adam
the handsomest man I'd ever seen.

Aunt Dorothy, green-visored, weak-eyed,
sat under a goose-neck lamp at a card table,
tinting black-and-white photographs.

My deaf grandmother puttered in the kitchen,
rattling bowls and baking tins, making another
lopsided two-layer caramel cake that might,
or might not, be done before the final scene of *Bonanza*.

My grandfather, small and fidgety,
sat at the upright piano,
and played, over and over, with one hand,
"When My Dreamboat Comes Home."

Uncle Glen wore a toupee.
He and my father
in red upholstered chairs
talked about the stock market
and the nutritional value of brewer's yeast.

My mother didn't speak. She sat alone,
still as a figurine, next to the shelf
with the antique Wedgwood, looking out
on to Washington Avenue.

What she saw, she never said.

Andrews Shopping Center: 1968

Back in the kitchen of my family's store,
the famous World War One aviator Ernie Hall
fries hamburgers in a skillet, opens a can
of Campbells' baked beans, serves it up
on thick white plates. Dinner for the workers.
Summer. Seven o'clock.

I stand behind the counter at the till, sweat
dampening my pits. Three more hours till closing.
My legs ache. Trumpets, drums, whistles,
the sounds of summer band
drift through the door wedged open
to a sticky Ohio twilight.

Customers wander the aisles,
looking for socket wrenches,
or nails, or bread, milk for breakfast,
a pack of Marlboros, copper fittings, or a gallon
of Sherwin Williams semi-gloss paint in French Vanilla.
If we don't have it, you don't need it, my uncle says.

I stamp prices on boxes of tacks,
purple ink staining my fingers,
restock the cigarettes,
calculate 4% sales tax on an order
of galvanized pipe. I wish I were anywhere
but at our store on a Saturday night in July.

It's too hot to eat Ernie's burgers and beans.
My father brings me a glass of lemonade,
slushy cold from the freezer.
He places his hand briefly on my shoulder,
then goes back to cutting glass and fixing screens,
singing as he always does when he works
the theme to *High Noon*.

Sometimes, even now, as the light fades,
and the evening quiets into night,
I catch the music from a passing car.
I hear his voice: "Do not forsake me, oh my darling."

Wisconsin Triolet: My Future Mother-in-Law Teaches Me to Play Sheepshead

At a table of skilled Sheepshead players, each card played is both a tactic and a statement. Sometimes the information carried by a card is more important than what the card actually achieves, and sometimes what the card achieves has little to do with the points it takes or gives. It is a game in which there is almost always a right play and a wrong play; few choices are indifferent.
—Control Group, Kuro5hin.org

In Sheepshead, you never know your partner
until the cards are played. See a Jack,
that's the partner. Lead trump if you're the partner,
fail if you're not. You never know the partner
until the cards are played. Sometimes it's smarter
to pick the cards. Sometimes you pass. Fact:
in Sheepshead, you never know your partner
until the cards are played. See the Jack?

In the blind? In your hand? Never tell.
Queens, Jacks, diamonds, carry weight, all are trump.
You'll never know your partner very well.
You picked up the Jack in the blind? Don't tell.
Listen, girl: playing cards is how we tell
if you belong. Aces, kings, and tens bump
up your points. Feeling blind? Never tell.
In Sheepshead, you'll need diamonds, you'll need trump.

Live Trap

Dear
Diane,
Can you get
this live trap through
Amazon for me?
You usually know how
to get things with free shipping:
www dot amazon dot
com/havahart/two-door-chipmunk-trap.
The chipmunks have been pesky since you've been
gone. The weather's fair, though we need some
rain. The grass is parched, the roses
wilting. I made a beer can
chicken on the grill. Yours
tastes better. I hope
you come home soon.
The house is
empty.
Ken

Dear
Ken, I
ordered the
havahart live
trap today. Reviews
on Amazon look good:
One man said he spray-painted
the chipmunks' tails, just like you do.
Only way to know you're not catching
the same chipper twice. It's sultry here and
hot. My writing goes well, but my dreams
are troubled. When I come home, we
can sit on the lawn, listen
to the brook, watch evening
settle across the
maples. The trap
will arrive
Monday.
Love,
D.

True Confessions

The high school marching band in late July:
sunburn, grass, the valve-oil scented air,
a Sousa march, all coalesced when I
first saw the brown-eyed boy who played the snare
drum, beating out spondees in four-four time.
Sixteen, his t-shirt tight across his chest,
he moved across the field, his body lithe,
his skin the color of ripe wheat. I confess
we kissed before I even knew his name.
His perfect hand, his breath...oh, I remember,
though it's mostly lies and partly pain.
Band, boy, summer: I dismember
facts and rearrange the truth (and so do you),
to tell a tale of love that's false, but true.

Sault Ste. Marie

Standing at the Soo,
you name for her the
laker coming light
from Huron, waiting
for its turn to slip into
the narrow passage,
almost like a prayer,
waiting for the rising waters
to lift it to Superior.

Later, when you lock
your arms around her,
slip yourself inside her,
you feel her body flow
like water, shaping
to your form, and lift your
weight with her rising,
lifting you to light,
almost like a prayer.

Aberdeen, Midwinter

Throughout the murky cave of winter night
in Aberdeen, we burrowed in the dark
like miners without lamps to guide our sultry
explorations. We scrabbled, hands and knees,
toward day. Our quaking limbs, soon taught the way
by toes and tongues and fingertips, could scarcely
keep apace our need for shelter in
the dark. We were so young, so young.
We still believed the weak midwinter sun
would rise trembling in the east, and we would
be transformed by love. Instead, we wakened
to a sunless dawn and sea birds' sad laments,
to thickening haar obscuring land and sky,
and North Sea waves pounding on the strand.

Haar on Don Street

Now it's been thirty years or more since I
last saw the haar slide off the sea, slink up
the hill through red-bricked streets. Three decades spent
since I last kissed the cool, damp fingers of
the northern sea, walked the cobblestones
of Aberdeen in streetlights' amber glow,
and passed through Seaton Park cocooned in mist.
So long ago I paused in sea-borne fog,
and thought I knew the course of days to come;
then climbed my wooded way to Don Street,
home for one brief year, and to the granite hall
where you, my love, stood silent at the door.
Through all my years, I see you still, your arms
outstretched, your face wreathed ghostly by the haar.

The Mathematics of Seeing You Again

Question 1:
If a plane leaves Detroit at 6:00 pm, traveling at the speed of light,
if the train from Ann Arbor to Chicago, on average,
runs five minutes late,
if you've been married twice and I have a husband,
if you have three children and I have two,
and if it's been seventeen years, two months and twelve days
since I saw you last, calculate,
my chances of seeing you again.

Question 2:
What additions and subtractions ought I make
to your picture, the one I keep locked
in my mind's eye?

Question 3:

$$x = -\frac{b}{2a}$$

For the parabola describing the years of our lives,
plot the axes of symmetry around which we twirl,
like dancers unable to touch,
moving in time to a slow minuet,
across the wide oceans of infinite space.

Question 4:

$$F_g = \frac{Gm_1 m_2}{r^2}$$

Using Newton's law of universal gravitation,
determine the velocity of bodies
falling into each other in the dark
on a warm, spring night.

Question 5:

$$M = \frac{y_1 - y_2}{x_1 - x_2}$$

Map for me the slope of your changing face,
the intimate topography of your body,
remind me of your secret geometry.

Extra Credit
In the new math of sudden
presence, solve for x
in our impossible equation.

"Shall I Compare Thee to a Summer's Day?" You Ask

Always one for questions, you. All right,
compare me to a summer's day, a hot
Ohio afternoon when storms rip southward
from Lake Erie, or sweep in from the western flatlands,
storms that land full force in my Mahoning Valley.
Make my voice a rumbling brontide,
or sudden crack that shakes the house.
Spray my body with *Parfum de Ozone*,
fill my eyes with pitch black anvil clouds.
Set my coif afire, give me hair
of sparking wire. Make me a twisting wind
that blows right off Fujita's scale. Dogs
will cower. This is what you had in mind?
Go ahead, compare away. Make my day.

February

February settles in like an unwelcomed guest,
noncommittal about the length of his visit.
He brings with him his smart-assed groundhog, and
one sunny day. February laughs at our hopes for spring.

Magazines at the grocery checkout line
tell us that we must build bikini bodies now,
but February whispers in our ears,
"Macaroni and cheese. Pot roast. Pie."

February bears strong-willed women:
Susan B. and me, we share our stars on
an empty-hearted day, February's bright spot over.
No wonder we're cranky; we were born

belatedly. Our moment comes on
a day of regret, a day of hangovers and
second thoughts, the cloying taste of cheap
chocolates thick on our tongues.

February strokes our hair, tells us to go back to bed,
bury our heads beneath blankets, like hibernating bears.
But Susan B. and me, we're two mean bitches.
We rip the hearts from our sleeves

(where they never belonged anyway)
and stare February down. So what if it's
fifteen below and still snowing? We grit our teeth,
and face the grinning lion on the doorstep.

Snatches

1.

Adrienne, you dove into your wreck
too soon. We need your sturdy voice
to rise above the clamor and the stink
of politics and greed. In Michigan the boys
in Lansing try to ban a woman's right
to speak because she dares to say vagina
in the chambers of the House. The fight
goes on. The Speaker's brief reminder
that decorum is required in the House
rings false. Instead the message reads: Unruly
women have no place outside a house;
or, women should be seen, not heard. Truly,
either way, it still comes out the same:
Shut your mouth and your vagina, dame.

2.

mouth
above
and below:
beware of teeth

3.

(Warning: Caution is advised. The following
may contain images and language not
suitable for children.)

(though last year two million
girl children endured female circumcision)

How to Circumcise a Girl

First: Find a girl.

Second: Confirm that she has reached puberty,
but is still a virgin. If she is not a virgin, skip
step three. Consider running over her with a car.[1]

Third: Make a choice. Remove the tip of her clitoris
or
remove the entire clitoris and labia
or
remove the clitoris and labia and sew up the vagina.

It all depends on how serious you are
about shutting her up.[2]

4.

Back cover praise for *The Medieval Chastity Belt: A Myth Making Process*, by Albrecht Classen, Palgrave McMillan, 2007:

"What a delight! With humor, erudition, and a fine sense of history's changing mind-sets, Classen takes the reader on a wonderful and surprising journey into a realm where academics often fear to tread. Many a modern scholar may be a bit chagrined by Classen's research and results, but wholly captivated; and the medievalist will surely smile." —G. Ronald Murphy, SJ, Georgetown University

5.

You know the film, it's black and white, a cheeky
mouthy woman spouting off, it could
be Hepburn, or Bacall, she's always lovely,
smart, and tall, all movie long a drawn-
out battle, wits and words, until the moment
when the hero kisses her full on the mouth
while she's midsentence

---

[1] Philip Caulfield and Michael Sheridan write in the February 23, 2011, *Daily News*, "An Iraqi man in Arizona accused of killing his daughter because she had become too westernized was convicted on Tuesday of second-degree murder. Faleh Hassan Almaleki was found guilty of running over his daughter, Noor Faleh Almaleki, with his SUV in October 2009."

[2] Dr. Trisha McNair notes in "Genital Mutilation," *BBC Health*, January 2011, www.bbc.co.uk., "So drastic is the mutilation involved in the latter operation that young brides have to be cut open to allow penetration on their wedding night and are customarily sewn up afterwards."

It's Not Over Till It's Over

It's not over till it's over,
but sometimes it's over
before it even begins.

Sometimes it's over,
and you, caught unawares,
have no idea

that the curtain has closed,
the train has left the station,
the ship has sailed,

and there you are,
left standing on the sidewalk,
alone, listening to the fat lady sing,

thinking you're watching
the opening number when
really it's the grand finale,

thinking like Tony that
something's coming,
when really Maria is singing

that weepy song
over his
dead body,

thinking that this time,
when Ilsa walks into Rick's,
it's for keeps,

thinking that this time,
Hamlet decides
to be,

thinking that this time,
the Trojans look
the gift horse in the mouth,

thinking that this time,
your life is not like all those
other worn-out stories

that are over
before they
ever begin.

Notes

St Machar's in the Rain (10)
The Cathedral Church of Saint Machar is located in Aberdeen, Scotland, on a site where Saint Machar established a site of worship in 580. Normans built a cathedral at the site in 1131, but virtually nothing of this building has survived. The present building was begun in the 13th century. Saint Machar's is technically not a cathedral, but rather is now part of the Church of Scotland, though it retains its name.

William Dunbar was a 15th century Scottish poet. His best-known poem is "Lament for the Makars." "Makar" is the Scots word for poet, and in this poem, Dunbar mourns the many poets who died in ages past. The refrain line of Dunbar's poem is *timor mortis conturbat me*, or "fear of death disturbs me."

Andrews Shopping Center, 1968 (14)
Ernie Hall knew the Wright Brothers, trained aviators during World War I, ran a flying school just up the road from our family store, and cooked lunches and dinners for the workers most days. (See http://www.erniehallaviationmuseum.org/#!ernie-hall/crp1 for a biography and more information about Ernie.)

Wisconsin Triolet: My Future Mother-in-Law Teaches Me to Play Sheepshead (15)
Sheepshead is a card game played obsessively in Wisconsin. The rules to the game are complicated and seemingly unending, as are the terms and expressions (often in German) used by players.

Sault Ste Marie (18)
The Soo Locks are located at Sault Ste Marie, in Michigan's Upper Peninsula.

Haar on Don Street (20)
Haar is a Scottish word for sea fog that rolls in off the North Sea on Scotland's east coast.

February (23)
Susan B. Anthony, the famous American suffragette, was born on February 15, 1820. I was born on the same day, one hundred and thirty-two years later.

Snatches (24)
In June 2010, Michigan State Representative Lisa Brown made a passionate speech on abortion on the floor of the Michigan Legislature. She finished the speech with these words: "And finally, Mr. Speaker, I'm flattered that you're all so interested in my vagina, but 'no' means 'no.'" At this point, Rep. Brown was banned from the floor and was not permitted to speak further on any bill. On the same day, Representative Barb Byrum was also banned from the floor for attempting to introduce an amendment to an abortion bill that would bar men from receiving vasectomies unless it was to save their lives. (See http://www.theguardian.com/world/2012/jun/15/michigan-politician-banned-using-word-vagina)

With Gratitude

Many thanks to friends who read and commented on the poems in this chapbook: Beth Myers, Shannon Castleton, Sarah Jane Baxter, Stephanie Roach, Janis Weakland, Dinah Wakeford, Bob Ploegstra and Michelle Ott. Thanks also to Miriam Gamble, Jack Ridl, Carol Ann Duffy, Dilys Rose, Brittany Perham and David Baker for their kind and helpful instruction. I am grateful for my time at Moniack Mhor, Scotland's Creative Writing Centre, located in the Highlands near Loch Ness, where several of these poems were composed and workshopped.

Special thanks to Char-Lene Wilkins for my photo, and to Don Cellini, who not only served as trusted reader and mentor, but who also created the lovely photograph for the cover of this chapbook.

Finally, love and thanks to my husband Ken Henningfeld, and my daughters Kate Fort and Anne Henningfeld. Their support means the world to me.

Diane Henningfeld was born and raised in Howland Corners, Ohio, next door to Andrews' Shopping Center, a general store owned and operated by her father David Andrews and his brother Harmon. In 1974 she moved permanently to Adrian, Michigan, where she has lived with her husband, Ken, ever since. She has two daughters, Kate Fort and Anne Henningfeld.

Henningfeld holds a B.A. from Adrian College; an M.A. from Eastern Michigan University; and a Ph.D. from Michigan State University. She also studied at the University of Aberdeen in Aberdeen, Scotland, and is currently enrolled in the MSc. in creative writing program at the University of Edinburgh, Scotland.

In addition to teaching literature at Adrian College, where she is now a professor emerita, she worked as a freelance writer for over fifteen years. As such, she compiled and edited over twenty-five nonfiction books for young adults on current and historical events. She is also the author of *Confronting Global Warming: Health and Disease* (2010) and *Confronting Global Warming: Nature and Wildlife* (2011), published by Greenhaven Press. Her poetry has appeared in *The Michigan Poet, Penwood Review, Storm Cellar*, and *Dunes Review*.

www.ingramcontent.com/pod-product-compliance
Lightning Source LLC
Chambersburg PA
CBHW060225050426
42446CB00013B/3180